House Cleaning Guide:

House Cleaning Secrets and Tips

By

Angela Pierce

Table of Contents

Introduction 5

Chapter 1. Bedroom 7

Chapter 2. Kitchen 10

Chapter 3. Bathroom 13

Chapter 4. Family Room/Living Room 16

Chapter 5. Laundry Room 18

Chapter 6. The Garage 19

Chapter 7. Basement 22

Chapter 8. Garbage Disposal 24

Chapter 9. Tips on Good Housekeeping 26

Final Words 29

Thank You Page 31

House Cleaning Guide: House Cleaning Secrets and Tips

By Angela Pierce

© Copyright 2014 Angela Pierce

Reproduction or translation of any part of this work beyond that permitted by section 107 or 108 of the 1976 United States Copyright Act without permission of the copyright owner is unlawful. Requests for permission or further information should be addressed to the author.

This publication is designed to provide accurate and authoritative information in regard to the subject matter covered. This work is sold with the understanding that the publisher is not engaged in rendering legal, accounting, or other professional services. If legal advice or other expert assistance is required, the services of a competent professional person should be sought.

First Published, 2014

Printed in the United States of America

Introduction

Housecleaning might be a very daunting task if you look at it in the whole entirety of it, especially if your house is quite big with many rooms to clean. Wouldn't it be better to leave it up to your housekeeper or someone else more capable of doing so? Yes, that would be possible but what if the task fell upon you to complete and there's no getting around it?

Then you better suit up, cleaning clothes I mean, and read up on these tips and tricks on proper housekeeping and how to effectively clean your house in a jiffy. There are several rooms in a house and these rooms need to be cleaned separately so here are the ways on how to clean them properly with the least amount of time needed and with all grounds covered.

Sectioning

The first thing you need to do is to divide the house per room and sometimes into sections for a better coverage and better time management. It would save you a lot of time if you lay out the rooms first then arrange them chronologically so you will know which one is first and where to go next. Let us explore these rooms and work on from there.

Chapter 1. Bedroom

Your bedroom is one of the most sacred places in the house for you so cleaning it the right way is very essential because it will radiate good sleep and an even better morning when you wake up.

Tips on keeping your bedroom clean:

Prevention is better than cure so start arranging 4 or 5 item every time you sit on your dresser and do your makeup and hair. You can toss out 4 or 5 items that you have not used for the past year or even the past 6 months. It can be some of your cosmetics, empty perfume bottles you just never had the time to throw away, balled up tissues you used, etc.

Clean under your bed at least twice a week or whenever you vacuum so that dust mites or bed bugs won't develop and creep onto your sheets. That's a scary thought!

Clean your sheets once every week. It is hygienic and refreshing to clean your sheets and pillowcases at least every week.

Clean your dresser, table-top, chair, or any other furniture in your room with disinfectant after vacuuming or sweeping the floor.

Don't stack too much books or reading material on your nightstand. Start restacking books you've already red into the bookshelves or put in boxes for recycling or donations.

If you can't thoroughly dust your room fixtures, use the upholstery attachment of your vacuum to clean window blinds and headboards. Another cool trick if your duster is not small enough to fit through the blinds for cleaning, use a sock to wipe them.

If you're always in a hurry and never find time to clean your sheets regularly because it takes time to take out the sheets and choose the best ones then putting them on the fixtures, it would be best that on the next time you clean your sheets, tuck in an extra one in there for the following week. That would save you tons of time the next time you need to change them.

When you have a television or a computer or laptop in the bedroom, use microfiber cloth material to clean the surfaces. It is a much efficient way to wipe off those smudges. And the next time you're on the phone and just lounging around, take out a tissue and wipe your mirrors.

For delicate furniture or room fixtures, use a blow dyer to dust them off gently.

Store Pledge mitts or microfiber cloths in your nightstand or drawers so you can quickly dust you headboards, dressers, etc.

Chapter 2. Kitchen

The kitchen is one of the dirtiest places in the house and it is one of the rooms that need to always be clean because it is where you prepare your food, you cook your food here and you also eat them in the kitchen or the dining area. There are lots of spaces, cabinets, nooks and crannies in the kitchen that you need to clean and disinfect so you better start from top to bottom and everywhere in between.

For some tips on keeping your kitchen clean, read up on the following:

Open the refrigerator and inspect the items inside. While doing that, grab items that are already past the expiration date or is close to it that you will not use before it expires. Take out almost empty bottles that would not ma even one serving and toss it in the garbage. Check your fruits and vegetables if they are still fresh for eating and if not, chuck them in the trash. Wipe down the outside of the refrigerator with a cloth that was dampened with water and soap. Clean as much as you can with the surface of the refrigerator then move it aside to vacuum underneath it. This will prevent the wires to be tangled with dust and cobwebs.

Sometimes you get packets of ketchup or take out items that you save for future use but never came, so time has come to throw them out. You don't need them rotting in your fridge and you probably have a whole bottle of ketchup so you will never use the packet ones anyway. Include the take out cups and boxes that you've stowed away in there but were never used for anything. They just take up space.

Whenever you see spills and food droppings on your refrigerator, wipe them off immediately and don't let them harden and get stuck there. It will be much harder to remove icy and hard messes.

Wipe finger markings off the kitchen cabinets and table as well as the refrigerator.

For your cabinets and cupboards, wipe them down with a microfiber cloth dampened of water and soap. Make sure to wipe to the direction of the grain. You might need to repeat this method a few times to remove all the dirt. Please do this with your stovetops and countertops as well.

Kitchens also have garbage cans that need to be cleaned always! So after you have disposed of the trash, disinfect your garbage cans with an all-purpose cleaner by wiping the inside and the outside of the can with a clean cloth. It would also be best of you hose it down with water and soap first before disinfecting.

For the sink, scrub it clean with an old toothbrush and an all-purpose cleaner.

For the floors, sweep the entire room with a soft broom, blow out dust using a blow dyer for the hard-to-reach corners and vacuum the remaining dust. If you have a tiled floor, wipe it with a floor mop dipped in water and detergent. Repeat the process until the entire room is cleaned.

Chapter 3. Bathroom

This is also one room that needs to be disinfected at all times. This is used by everybody in the household making it one of the dirtiest parts of the house as well. It would be very hygienic and recommended to disinfect your bathroom everyday or at least the toilet.

Here are some more tips in keeping this haven clean and healthy for everybody:

After everyone has showered, brushed their teeth and have gotten ready for school or bed, wipe the mirrors and bathroom faucets with a dry terrycloth hand towel or any clean towel that's water absorbent. This will prevent mold build up and would make it easier to clean every day.

After showering, take a squeegee and clean the tub or stall tiles. Spread the shower curtain after use to prevent water from building up on the folds and create molds.

Use disposable makeup cloths that you've used to remove your makeup to wipe the counter, sink and floor. Make sure to rinse the makeup off the cloth first before using it on the bathroom tiles.

Since you'd want to keep your floors clean every day, store disposable cloths and floor duster on the cabinets for easy use when you clean it in the morning. Air prevents mildew and mold build up, so if you have a window in your bathroom, open it wide, especially in the mornings and let the air circulate and the sunshine in to decrease moisture.

You can also prevent mildew by mixing 10 parts of water to 1 part bleach; use a soft-bristled brush to clean your tiles. You can follow it up with a pH-balanced cleaner to flush the bleach solution.

When using oil-based products for your bath, make sure to clean your tub with warm water and a light cleanser to get rid of bathtub rings.

For your toilet, after flushing, spray ¼ cup of baking soda into the wet toilet bowl then scrub after taking a shower. Flush it again to rinse it off.

It is good to clean the pipes in your bathroom every month or two to prevent build up and clogging. Do this by pouring ½ cup baking soda down the drain and follow it up with ½ cup of white vinegar. It will foam up so let it foam for a several minutes and after that pour boiling water down the drain to flush out clogs.

Soap can also cause of dirt in your bathroom so get rid of soap scum with a solution of white vinegar and water. Take care in handling this mixture and make use of gloves when sprinkling it on your tiles. Rinse thoroughly afterwards.

Regularly wash your shower curtains. You can toss them in the washing machine then scrub it afterwards and let it air dry under the sun. If you cannot use a washing machine with it, use a solution of 10 parts water and 1 part bleach and scrub it down.

De-clog your showerheads. When you use certain products in your showers, it might clog your showerheads over time, so take time to clean them too.

Wash bathroom toys that your kids use for bathing. Even toys might develop mildew and molds.

Chapter 4. Family Room/Living Room

The family room is the room where everybody gets a part in. You hang out here with your family members and also friends who come over. There are lots of places where germs and dirt can hide in your family room so you also have to clean this room every week to prevent germs from developing.

Get some tips from the list below and learn to clean your family room effectively:

Vacuum the whole room making sure you also get the spaces under the sofas, tables and chairs.

Vacuum lampshades or use a blow dryer to delicate fixtures.

Dust off your bookshelves by using the upholstery attachment in your vacuum or you can blow dry the dirt from the corners to flush them out.

Get rid of old newspapers, magazines, or other reading material that are outdated and cannot be stored. For books and other magazines, store in the bookshelves or in boxes for donations.

Clear clutter by picking up tiny pieces of knick knacks around the room. Get a basket or container as you tour the room to out the unnecessary things in.

If you have kids and their toys are lying around the living room, grab them and put them in water with dishwashing paste to clean. Rinse with water thoroughly and wipe clean. It would be great if you have a closed container/storage for your kids' toys/

Clean artificial flowers or plants with the upholstery attachment of your vacuum cleaner.

If you have a wooden/concrete/tiles floor, sweep it clean then wipe with it a mop taking extra time on door entrances where dirt might build up.

For sofa pillows, aside from washing them every week, you can keep them fresh from mites and molds by putting them in the dyer on air cycle. Just pop 2 or 3 in there to toss and turn for a while.

Spot clean your walls by scrubbing any food stains or dirt build up especially in areas where your kids usually play in.

Make sure to clean thoroughly all the nooks and crannies by going underneath, above and below your furniture using a long-handled duster. Make sure to also clean the floor underneath your carpets.

Chapter 5. Laundry Room

Although the mother of the house is the usual person in the laundry room, it will still be beneficial to clean your space.

Here are some helpful tips to do so:

To avoid build up of laundry for your weekend laundry trips, try to do some batches within the week with some towels or other clothes.

Before popping your laundry in the tub, wipe it clean with a damp cloth. Wipe all the sides both inside and out and even the dyer then wash the cloth. Remove any residue in the filter.

Organize your laundry according to uses example, shirts go together, so does jeans, pants, etc. Presort them before putting them in so you can use your time efficiently.

Sort fresh laundry before putting in cabinets. For sheets and matching pillow cases, fold the pillowcases inside the sheet and flatten. Roll into one and stack on the shelves. It would be easier to grab and lay it out on the bed instead of going through your drawers one by one to find the matching pairs.

Chapter 6. The Garage

The garage is a big place to clean all by yourself or at least clean in a day. It's better to get the family in with this project, especially Dad, because there might be some heavy lifting going on here. There would be numerous clutters lying around in your garage where some can still be used while others not any longer. So the first thing to do in cleaning out your garage is to sort.

Aside from that, there are still a few that might be useful such as:
Sorting the junk from the ones you would like to keep or is still useful. In this time and age where corporate media makes us buy stuff we don't actually need, the garages are the Bermuda triangles of the modern family. It's where stuff go when there's no more space inside the house or you can't think of a use at that time, and it never seems to come out of the garage ever. So take the whole weekend to clean your garage because it is going to take a while.
Organize the stuff you've sorted out into different boxes for different uses, for example, a box where you

put in your donations, a box that will go directly to the trash and never come back, and another box for keeps.

Use plastic boxes for stuff you will keep in your garage and label them in categories such as Christmas items, old toys, pictures, etc.

Store those boxes in tall shelves. This will help save space in your garage and will look tidier and cleaner.

Do your duties with the other boxes such as recycling, donating, or giving to others. Just make sure it doesn't find its way back into your garage.

Take out large items from the garage such as tables, chairs or other furniture that has no use anymore. Do a garage sale with those items.

Once all clutter and items are organized and set aside, vacuum the entire garage, blowing out dust and dirt from corners and hard to reach places. Sometimes, when the garage is empty, you can use a powerful hose to hose down dirt from the walls and flush put dirt and grime.

Use an all-purpose cleaner in mopping down the walls and the floor and rinse with water thoroughly.

Use a car freshener to keep the garage smelling fresh or spray on disinfectant every few days to get rid of unwanted smell.

Hose down the floor every few days especially in rainy weather where the car tires might stain the floor with dirt.

Chapter 7. Basement

Just like the garage, this is a place where you store stuff you don't want inside the house or living room. Or a place where you put things that don't fit in any other place in your house. This is a daunting task but with the right tools and knowledge, you'll be done in a jiffy.

You will need:
Sponges
White vinegar
Cloths and rags
Dishwashing liquid
Ammonia
Rubbing alcohol
Vacuum, broom, mop
Baking soda
Pan
Batteries

Steps:

Gather all cleaning products and remove covers from your basement stuff. Give them a shake and out in the washing machine.

Wipe down the furniture that were stored or just get rid of it if there seems to be no use of them anymore.

Wipe down the water heater and furnace with warm water with suds.

Keep the area around your furnace and hot-water heater clean and clear of any clutters.

Dust your light bulbs and replace them if they are no longer working.

Mix 1 gallon of warm water, 1 cup of ammonia and 1 tsp of dishwashing liquid in a bucket. Do not mix ammonia with bleach.

Put draw cloths on the floor and dip your sponge into the bucket to wash down the walls.

Wash your windows too if you have any.

Sprinkle the floor with baking soda to neutralize any smells or odors then vacuum or sweep along with the stairs. Sweep from the corners towards the center of the room using long strokes.

Vacuum smoke detectors and replace their batteries for better performance.

Mop the floor with water and some soap.

Chapter 8. Garbage Disposal

Disposing garbage might probably the least wanted job in the world but everybody has to dispose their garbage properly to keep our environment clean and healthy for the next generations to come. You can start helping the planet by starting at home. Sort out your garbage and label them correctly for proper disposal. You can label into ones that you can recycled or re-use, biodegradable, and non-biodegradable. Do not burn your garbage. Burning your garbage in your backyard will only drill holes into the ozone layer especially if you burn plastic. Plus is will generate a lot of smoke and fumes. You wouldn't want your neighbors to complain against you.

Types:

Recycled/Re-use- these things are items that can be used again or things you can donate for other uses. It would be great to label them accordingly so the collector would know exactly what to do with them. If you prefer to donate them, you can send or take them directly to donation places for people in need or victims of natural disasters.

Biodegradable- biodegradable waste as described by the web is a type of waste which can be broken down into its base compounds, in a span of time, by micro-organisms and other living things, regardless of what those compounds may be. These items tend to rot and have mold build up so dispose of these things first and do it every day to avoid having smelly kitchens and contaminated space.

Non-biodegradable- this is the complete opposite of biodegradable waster meaning it cannot be broken down to its original form anymore. These wastes can last up to a few years without decomposing. These wastes are the ones that are slowly destroying the environment because of how they are not disposed properly.

Chapter 9. Tips on Good Housekeeping

Avoid anything left on the floor or dumped in the living room or anywhere in the house if it has no business being there. Pick up that candy wrapper or those dirty clothes and put them in the trash or dirty laundry bin. A small effort goes a long way when it comes to keeping the house clean and clutter-free.

Keep things in place. Make sure books are in the bookshelves and pillows on the sofa and not the other way around. Keep things in their right places at all times to avoid having to rearrange everything. This makes it easier to find things and to store things as well.

Everybody has to have their designated cleaning assignments, it might be a little tidying up task, or a sweeping task or a scrubbing task, when you out them all together, and it's a well-oiled cleaning household.

Make sure to clean up after yourself. You don't have a helper to follow you around all day and clean up after you so keep your stuff clean and anything you use, you clean right away.

When doing house chores or errands around the house, turn up some music, dance and have fun cleaning. When your spirits are up, you can cover more places to clean and have a happy disposition doing it.

Other Cleaning hacks to keep in mind:

Always keep a bottle filled with cleanser and paper towels in the kitchen and bathroom for easy cleaning quick fixes.

Put cleansers and other cleaners in a plastic bag or container so you can easily tote them around the places you need to clean.

Always try to clean each room everyday even for quick periods of time; this will make it easier for you when the general cleaning time comes around.

Don't do all things at once. Do one task at a time and finish your tasks first before going to another, otherwise, you'll never get anything done.

For a lampshade that's pleated, use a paintbrush to dust the dirt or vacuum it with the dust-brush attachment.

For flat lampshades, you can use a lint roller to remove the dust and dirt or use a blow dyer to remove dirt. Just set it on high and it will blow those dust away.

To prevent dirt and dust on you floor, try to make use of socks or shoe plastic covers when entering the house or at least in your bedroom.

Final Words

Cleaning out your house for the month or for the week is a hard task to tackle especially if you try doing it on your own. If you have a small house , probably with 2 bedrooms, a functional kitchen, living room and 2 bathrooms, then you can definitely clean it on your own if you are given the whole weekend to do it but not in a day because there are lots to consider and do when cleaning. Now if you have a bigger house with more rooms than 2, then you might need the help of other family members especially for the lifting and hoisting of heavy stuff.

Just keep in mind these simple tips in cleaning and you will get those tasks done in no time. Since it is outlined here how to go about it on every part of the house or at least every possible room in the house, it would be easier to decide what to do first and what would come next. It will boil down to your priorities, which one should go first, and the second and the third. For me, the gravity of the task will come into play when I am faced with where to clean first. I would think of the easiest room to clean and go for it then the second most likely to clean easier and so forth. You do not have to tackle them all at once. That would be time consuming and tiring because you will be running from room to room trying to finish them all at the same time when it is impossible for one person to clean the house in just a short span of time.

So keep smiling and be happy with whatever task you are given, whether it be cooking, washing, or cleaning the house. The house that is clean also represents the people living inside of it so if your house is dirty and cluttered, then you better look at your life and start cleaning up. It's never too late to start being a tidy and clean person. If your house is clean and free of garbage, your mood and outlook in life will also be the same, clean and gull of promise. So happy sorting and cleaning!

Thank You Page

I want to personally thank you for reading my book. I hope you found information in this book useful and I would be very grateful if you could leave your honest review about this book. I certainly want to thank you in advance for doing this.

www.ingramcontent.com/pod-product-compliance
Lightning Source LLC
LaVergne TN
LVHW021747060526
838200LV00052B/3514